TIME TRAVEL GUIDES

ANCIENT ROME

John Malam

www.raintree.co.uk/library
Visit our website to find out more information about

To order:
☎ Phone 44 (0) 1865 888112
🖹 Send a fax to 44 (0) 1865 314091
💻 Visit the Raintree bookshop at www.raintree.co.uk/library to browse our catalogue and order online.

First published in Great Britain by Raintree, Halley Court, Jordan Hill, Oxford OX2 8EJ, part of Harcourt Education. Raintree is a registered trademark of Harcourt Education Ltd.

© Harcourt Education Ltd 2008
First published in paperback in 2008
The moral right of the proprietor has been asserted.

Editorial: Sarah Shannon, Lucy Beevor,
  and Harriet Milles
Adaptation for Freestyle Express: Sarah Levete
  and Geoff Barker
Design: Steve Mead, Geoff Ward, and Ian Winton
Picture Research: Ruth Blair
Illustrations: Eikon Illustration, Tim Slade
  and Jeff Edwards
Production: Duncan Gilbert

Originated by Modern Age
Printed and bound in China by South China Printing Company Ltd.

ISBN 978 1 4062 0859 7 (hardback)
12 11 10 09 08
10 9 8 7 6 5 4 3 2 1

ISBN 978 1 4062 0866 5 (paperback)
12 11 10 09 08
10 9 8 7 6 5 4 3 2 1

British Library Cataloguing in Publication Data
Malam, John, 1957-
Ancient Rome. - (Time travel guides)
1. Rome - Civilization - Juvenile literature
937
A full catalogue record for this book is available from the British Library.

Acknowledgements
The publishers would like to thank the following for permission to reproduce photographs:
©AKG images **pp. 16, 26** (Erich Lessing), **43** (Gilles Mermet), **24, 35** (Nimatallah), **15, 34** (Peter Connolly), **9** (Pirozzi); ©Ancient Art & Architecture Collection Ltd. **pp. 14, 28, 32, 33, 50–51, 52**; ©Art Archive **pp. 49** (Archaeological Museum, Corinth/Dagli Orti), **20–21, 44–45, 54–55** (Bibliothèque des Arts Décoratifs, Paris/Dagli Orti); **10, 23, 38–39** (Dagli Orti), **19** (Musée de la Civilisation Gallo-Romaine, Lyons/Dagli Orti), **46** (Museo Civico, Padua/Dagli Orti), **6–7, 11, 40, 42, 53** (Museo della Civilta Romana, Rome/Dagli Orti), **26–27** (Museo Nazionale, Palazzo Altemps, Rome/Dagli Orti), **36** (Archaeological Museum, Madrid/Dagli Orti), **8** (Archaeological Museum, Naples/Dagli Orti), **12** (Cathedral Museum, Ferrara/Dagli Orti), **30–31** (Galleria Borghese, Rome/Dagli Orti), **25** (Jan Vinchon Numismatist, Paris/Dagli Orti), **17** (Museo Prenestino, Palestrina/Dagli Orti); ©Corbis **pp. 29** (Araldo de Luca), **18** (Roger Wood).

Cover photograph of the Colosseum in Rome reproduced with permission of Corbis/Richard T. Nowitz. Portrait of the lawyer Terentius Neo and his wife reproduced with permission of Werner Forman Archive/Museo Archeologico Nazionale, Naples. Photograph of the head of Octavian (Augustus) reproduced with permission of Ancient Art & Architecture Collection Ltd./Prisma.

The publishers would like to thank Michael Vickers for his assistance in the preparation of this book.

Every effort has been made to contact copyright holders of any material reproduced in this book. Any omissions will be rectified in subsequent printings if notice is given to the publishers.

CONTENTS

Words that appear in the text in bold, **like this**, are explained in the Glossary.

N
W · E
S

River Tiber

THE PANTHEON

THEATRE OF MARCELLUS

FORUM

THE COLOSSEUM

TIBERINA
ISLAND

CIRCUS MAXIMUS

BATHS OF CARACALLA

MAP OF ANCIENT ROME

Britain

Northern
Europe

France

Spain

Rome

Africa

Mediterranean Sea

ROMAN EMPIRE

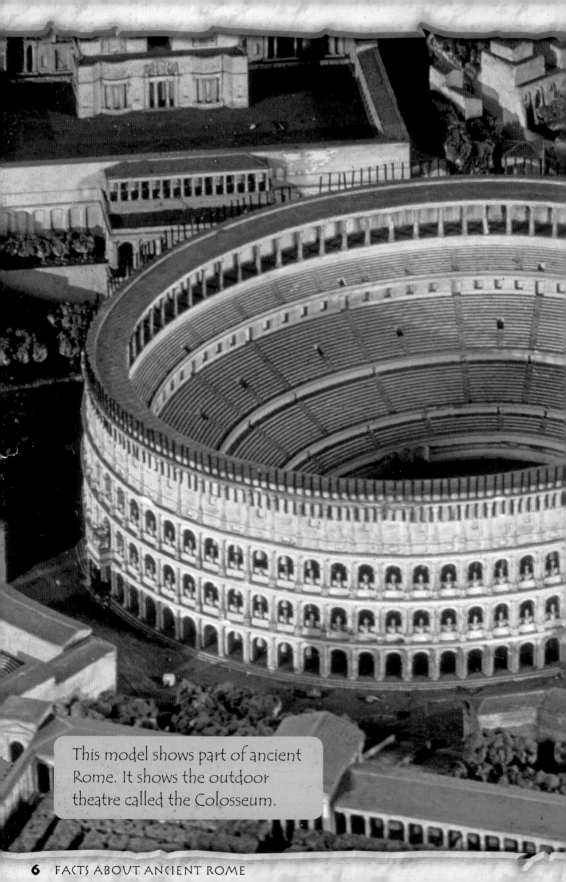

This model shows part of ancient Rome. It shows the outdoor theatre called the Colosseum.

CHAPTER 1

FACTS ABOUT ANCIENT ROME

You are about to go on the trip of a lifetime. You are travelling to the city of ancient Rome. This is in the country of Italy.

Prepare to travel about 1,700 years back in time. You are going to the early 4th century.

People speak in Latin. This is the language of the Romans. An ancient Roman may greet you, saying "*Salve, hospes!*" (Hello, stranger!). Smile and say "*Salve*" (Hello).

THE BIRTH OF A GREAT CITY

You will arrive in ancient Rome around AD 300. That is 1,700 years ago. AD means the start of the modern calendar. That was 2,000 years ago! But how did this great city begin? There are many stories about the beginnings of Rome.

AENEAS, FATHER OF THE ANCIENT ROMAN PEOPLE

Many people believe that a brave **warrior** is the father of ancient Rome. He is called Aeneas. He fought in many battles. Aeneas's own city of Troy had been destroyed. Someone told him that one day he would eat the plate his food was served on. This is where he would live.

Aeneas arrived in the country of Italy. It was usual in ancient Rome to use bread as a plate. Aeneas ate the bread – this was his plate! Aeneas settled in Italy. Ancient Romans believe he is their **ancestor** (ancient family member).

A man removes an arrow from Aeneas' leg. ✔

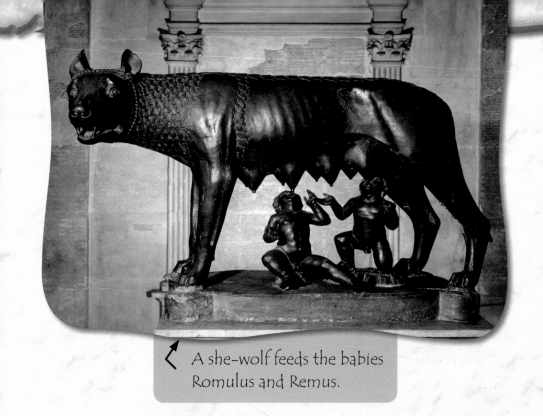

A she-wolf feeds the babies
Romulus and Remus.

ROMULUS AND REMUS

Another story is about two boys. A cruel king called
Amulius tried to drown them. The boys were his
relatives. They were twins called Romulus and
Remus. But a she-wolf rescued them. She fed them
with her own milk. Later, a shepherd looked after
the boys.

One day, Romulus killed King Amulius. The twins
built a city on a hill beside the River Tiber. But the
twins argued. Romulus killed Remus. The city was
named Rome after Romulus.

THE BUSY CAPITAL

This road is the Via Appia. It leads to Rome.

Rome is the capital of the Roman **Empire**. The empire is a group of countries ruled by Rome. It covers much of west Europe. It covers parts of central Europe. It also covers parts of north Africa and east Asia. About 50 million people live in the Roman Empire.

About one million people live in the city of ancient Rome. Most live here all the time. Some are visitors from other countries. Like you, they are tourists. Others come to Rome on business.

LOTS OF DIFFERENT PEOPLE

Rome is a **multicultural** city. This means that lots of different people live here. Many people come from other countries, such as Britain and France. They speak different languages. But Latin is the main language of the Roman Empire.

GETTING TO ANCIENT ROME

It's easy to get to ancient Rome. Travel on foot. Or you can go by horse or carriage. Keep to the main roads – they all lead to Rome. About 80,000 km (50,000 miles) of roads cross the empire.

Do visit the Roman **Forum** (see page 22). This is an open space for public meetings. Take a look at the Golden Milestone. This is a gold-covered column. It is carved with the names of the empire's main cities. It shows their distances from Rome. Work out how far you have travelled!

ANCIENT ROME STREET MAP

Look at the town plan. This plan is called the *Forma Urbis*. It is fixed to the wall on the Temple of Peace. The plan is very detailed.
It will help you get around the city.
The picture shows a small
piece of the plan.

WHEN TO VISIT

Go to Rome at festival time. Festivals are held in honour of Roman gods and goddesses. They are holidays for everyone. People relax and have fun. There are over 150 festival days each year!

THE FESTIVAL OF SATURNALIA

The Festival of Saturnalia is in honour of the god Saturn. The festival takes place in December. It lasts for a week. On the first day an animal is **sacrificed** (killed). This is a gift for Saturn. People offer gifts to the gods. They believe gifts keep the gods happy (see page 27).

On the last day, there is a fair. People give small presents to each other. They buy them from the market at the fair.

This is a pottery figure of the god Saturn. Presents like this may be given during the festival.

MODERN LINKS

The Festival of Saturnalia is linked to the modern world. Leaders of the Christian Church later turned it into a Christian festival. This celebrates the birth of Jesus Christ. This happens on 25th December.

THE FESTIVAL OF PARILIA

The festival of Parilia is held in April. It is in honour of Rome's birthday. People ask the gods to protect farmers and animals.

THE WEATHER IN ANCIENT ROME

Seasons

Spring (March–May): warm and showery

Summer (June–August): very hot and dry

Autumn (September–November): warm and rainy

Winter (December–February): cold

Average daytime temperature

January: 5°C–11°C

July: 20°C–30°C

September: 17°C–26°C

Average rainfall

January: 71 mm

July: 15 mm

September: 63 mm

Average days of sunshine

January: 7 sunny days out of 31

July: 26 sunny days out of 31

September: 24 sunny days out of 30

Average days of rain

January: 8 rainy days out of 31

July: 1 rainy day out of 31

September: 5 rainy days out of 30

WHERE TO STAY

It's easy to find somewhere
to stay. But you may
have a nasty surprise.
Some houses are in
poor condition.

PLACES TO STAY

If you're short of money,
rent an apartment.
These are in housing
blocks. There is no
running water and
nowhere to cook. The
toilets are quite smelly
(see box on page 15). The
housing blocks are overcrowded.
They are noisy and dirty. Fire
and disease spread quickly.

The rooms of
a house are set
around a private
garden.

ANCIENT ROMAN HOMES

If you have lots of money, rent a house. It will have
several bedrooms and a dining room. You can cook
food in the fireplace. There is a well in the garden.
Here, you can get fresh water. The house will be clean
and comfortable. It is the opposite of an apartment.

GOING TO THE TOILET

In a house, empty your **chamber pot** (toilet bowl) into a hole in the garden. In an apartment, use one of the block's toilet pipes. Watch out. Hundreds of other people use them too. The smell from the pipes is awful.

BENEATH THE CITY STREETS

The city's main **sewer** (underground drain) runs under the streets. The sewer flushes the waste from the toilets into the River Tiber. (Don't swim there!)

There are no doors in public toilets! ↗

FOOD AND DRINK

There are many bars and restaurants in the city. Buy a hot snack such as a spicy sausage. There are lots of bakeries. Buy some sweet cakes and pastries. They are made with lots of honey.

Ancient Romans often miss breakfast. Instead they eat a snack. This may be bread, cheese, fruit, and water. The midday meal is also small. This is meat or fish with bread. The main meal is at about 3 p.m. Special feasts last for several hours. These are called **banquets** (see box on page 17).

WINE AND WATER

People drink lots of wine. Wine is mixed with water. It is flavoured with herbs or honey. There are many fountains in the city. You can drink fresh water from these.

This picture shows a man selling fruit and vegetables.

✎ A musician will entertain you during the banquet.

TABLE MANNERS

This is the polite way to behave at a banquet:

- Lie on a couch around the table.
- Lie on your left side. Lean on your elbow.
- Before the meal and between each course, wash your hands. Or let a servant do this for you.
- When you are full, belch and break wind.
- After the meal, stay for games and songs.

BANQUET MENU

Starter
- shellfish
- oysters in garlic sauce
- snails in their shells
- boiled eggs
- olives
- figs
- sweet wine

Main course
- roast boar stuffed with sausages and egg yolks
- stuffed dormice in honey sauce
- peacocks
- fish
- cabbage
- wine

Dessert
- fresh fruit
- nuts
- cakes
- honeyed wine

WHAT TO WEAR

Rich and poor people dress differently in ancient Rome. So think carefully about what you wear.

CLOTHES FOR MEN AND BOYS

In the 4th century, most men and boys wear tunics. These are strips of material. They are worn like dresses. Tunics are often made from wool. This can feel itchy! Wealthy people wear tunics made from soft silk. Some tunics are plain. Others are decorated with a purple stripe.

TOGAS

The man seated in the picture wears a **toga**. This is a loose cloak. It wraps around the body.

Wear leather sandals indoors. Wear leather ankle boots outside. Slaves wear wooden-soled shoes such as clogs.

FASHION FOR WOMEN AND GIRLS

Women wear tunics. These are plain or stripy. Women wear leather shoes. The shoes are soft and coloured red. Wealthy women fasten jewels to their shoes! Women don't wear hats. In the rain, they pull their cloaks over their heads.

HAIR

Beards are not in fashion. Criminals may have beards. **Criminals** are people like thieves. People in mourning may also have beards. They are sad because someone has died.

Women comb their hair back. They tie it up in a bun. Blonde is the most fashionable hair colour.

Roman women often wear long earrings.

All ancient Roman roads meet in the Forum.

CHAPTER 2

WHERE TO GO

There's so much to see in ancient Rome!
In the city, there are:
- 11 town squares
- 11 large bathhouses
- 856 smaller bathhouses
- 10 **basilicas** (shopping centres)
- 28 libraries.

Begin sightseeing in the Roman **Forum**. This square is the centre of ancient Rome. Walk from here to the shops and markets. And make sure you visit the Pantheon building. This is a **temple**. It is built to honour all the Romans' gods and goddesses.

THE ROMAN FORUM

The Roman **Forum** is sometimes called the Great Forum – but it's a small space! It is only 100 metres by 70 metres.

The Forum is the centre of ancient Rome. A forum is a city square. Here **politicians** make speeches. Politicians are people who run the country. Large feasts called **banquets** are held here. Religious events are held here.

There are many buildings around the Forum. These include **basilicas** (shopping centres). There are many columns in these buildings.

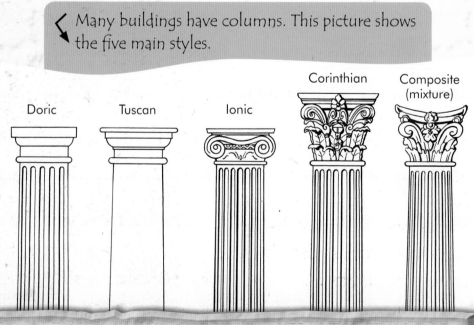

Many buildings have columns. This picture shows the five main styles.

Doric   Tuscan   Ionic   Corinthian   Composite (mixture)

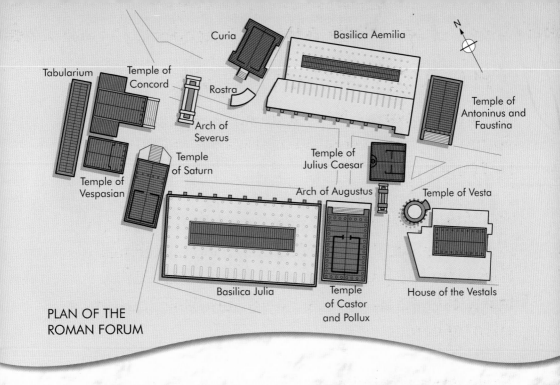

Curia

Basilica Aemilia

N

Tabularium

Temple of Concord

Rostra

Arch of Severus

Temple of Antoninus and Faustina

Temple of Saturn

Temple of Julius Caesar

Temple of Vespasian

Arch of Augustus

Temple of Vesta

Basilica Julia

Temple of Castor and Pollux

House of the Vestals

PLAN OF THE ROMAN FORUM

THE TEMPLE OF VESTA

This ancient temple or religious building is in the Forum. It was built for the goddess Vesta. She protects peoples' homes.

Most Roman temples are in a rectangle shape. The Temple of Vesta is round. This reminds ancient Romans of their **ancestors**. Ancestors are family members who lived in the past. They lived in round huts.

You can see that the Temple of Venus has Corinthian columns.

This stone sculpture shows customers buying pillows and materials.

SHOPS AND MARKETS

There are lots of places where you can spend your money. There are shops on the ground floor of the city's housing blocks (see page 14). The shops sell bread, wine, meat, and fish. They sell pots, pans, and lamps. At the back of the shops, shopkeepers make or store their goods.

On the pavements, farmers set up stalls (tables). Here you can buy fresh fruit and vegetables.

For special items, visit one of the city's squares. Here you can buy gold and silver jewellery, and perfume.

MONEY AND MONEYLENDERS

Pay for your shopping with gold or bronze coins. Make sure you use the right ones! In the early 4th century, only use coins picturing the ruler, **Emperor** Constantine. There are lots of other coins too. These have pictures of earlier emperors.

You can borrow money from a moneylender. But watch out. He will ask you to pay the money back. Then he will add on an extra amount. You may end up in debt. This means you owe lots of money. And it is hard to pay it back.

Roman coins show the head of the ruling emperor.

THE PANTHEON

Try to visit the Pantheon. This is a **temple**. It is built to honour all the gods and goddesses of ancient Rome. It was built 1,890 years ago!

The roof is shaped like the top half of a ball. It is 43 metres from the ground. Daylight pours in through a wide hole in the centre of the roof. This hole is often called the "eye" of the temple.

Look up to the "eye" of the Pantheon.

HOUSES FOR THE GODS

The ancient Romans believe gods and goddesses are powerful beings. They believe that they control daily life (see box on page 27). A temple is a god's home on Earth. Inside, there is a **sacred** (holy) statue. The ancient Romans believe that the god's spirit lives inside the statue.

People leave gifts for the gods at their temples. They hope that in return the gods will look after them. Some gifts are crumbs of bread. Others are goats or sheep.

ROMAN GODS AND GODDESSES

Some of the most important gods and goddesses are:

- **Apollo** – god of prophecy (telling the future) and healing
- **Juno** – goddess of women and marriage; queen of the gods, married to Jupiter
- **Jupiter** – god of the heavens and weather; king of the gods, married to Juno
- **Mars** – god of war
- **Neptune** – god of the oceans (see picture on right)
- **Venus** – goddess of love
- **Vesta** – goddess of the home
- **Vulcan** – god of fire

CHRISTIANS WELCOME!

For hundreds of years, Roman rulers did not let people follow the Christian religion. But about 1,700 years ago, Emperor Constantine allowed Christians to practise their religion. They can celebrate the life of Jesus Christ.

HAVE A GOOD BATH

There are many places to wash and relax in ancient Rome. These are called baths. Here you can relax with a massage. You can swim in the pools. The baths are also great places to meet friends.

THE BATHS OF CARACALLA

The Baths of Caracalla are the grandest in Rome. They are a huge set of buildings.

Make sure you go at the correct time. Women and older people use the baths in the morning. So do people with disabilities. Men use the baths in afternoon.

PEOPLE WHO WORK IN THE BATHS

- Changing room helpers look after your clothes.
- Hair-removers cut and shave your hair.
- Body-scrapers clean your body with oil.
- Massage experts rub oils into your body.
- Perfume sellers sell oils. These make you smell nice.

Fill a flask with oil to use at the baths.

CENTRAL HEATING

The Baths of Caracalla are warm. Heat comes from tunnels. The tunnels run beneath the floors. They also run behind the walls of the baths.

The tunnels fill with hot air. This comes from fires. The hot air heats the water. This makes steam for the sweat rooms. This keeps the building warm.

This photograph shows the ruins of the Baths of Caracalla.

VISITING ANCIENT ROMAN BATHS

1. First, go to the *apodyterium* (the changing room). Take off your clothes.
2. Go to the *sudatorium*. This is a small room. Here, hot steam will make you sweat.
3. Go to the *caldarium*. In this hot room, rub warm oil into your skin. Scrape it off with a strigil (scraper). Or a body-scraper can do this for you.
4. Go to the *tepidarium*. Soak yourself in the warm pool.
5. Go to the *frigidarium*. Now jump into this room's cold pool. Have a swim.
6. Go to the *unctuarium*. Have a massage with perfumed oils. Then get dressed.
7. Relax – buy something to eat. Have a chat with friends.

Ancient Romans enjoy watching gladiator fights.

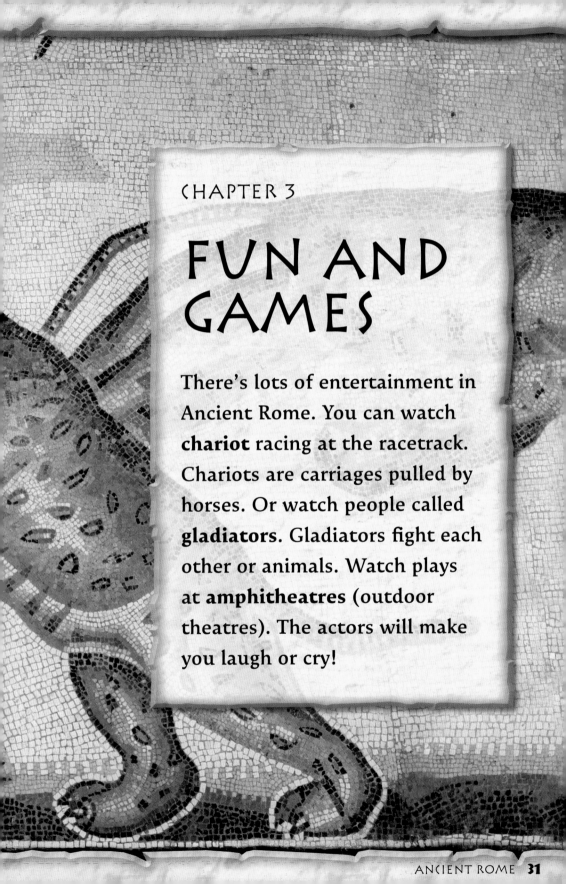

CHAPTER 3

FUN AND GAMES

There's lots of entertainment in Ancient Rome. You can watch **chariot** racing at the racetrack. Chariots are carriages pulled by horses. Or watch people called **gladiators**. Gladiators fight each other or animals. Watch plays at **amphitheatres** (outdoor theatres). The actors will make you laugh or cry!

These modern houses are built on top of the ruins of the Theatre of Marcellus.

OFF TO THE THEATRE!

Ancient Romans like the theatre. The theatres are open-air buildings. They are in the shape of a semi-circle. Men play all the parts. They even play the parts of women.

ANCIENT ROME'S THEATRES

Campus Martius is the main theatre area. You can visit three theatres. These are the Theatre of Pompey, the Theatre of Balbus, and the Theatre of Marcellus. They are all free.

The Theatre of Marcellus is Rome's best theatre. 20,000 people can fit in. Performances are in the afternoon. Arrive early to get a seat. The stone seats are very uncomfortable. Take a soft cushion.

Make sure you sit in the correct place. Women sit at the back. Men sit towards the front. The front row seats are only for important people. The **emperor** (ruler) and rich people sit here.

CLAP OR HISS?

What did you think of the play?
- You liked the play – clap your hands.
- You loved the play – wave a handkerchief in the air.
- You hated the play – throw apples or figs. Or boo and hiss!

ACTORS AND PLAYS

Actors wear masks and clothes.

- Happy masks are for comedy.
- Sad masks are for **tragedy**.
- Brown masks show the actor is playing a man.
- White masks show the actor is playing a woman.
- White clothes show the actor is playing a young person.
- Coloured clothes show the actor is playing an elderly person.
- Purple clothes show the actor is playing a rich person.
- Red clothes show the actor is playing a poor person.

This mask shows the actor is playing a man in a comedy.

CHEER THE CHARIOTS!

Chariots are carriages pulled by horses. Watch chariot racing and horse racing in circuses. These are racetracks. The biggest racetrack is the Circus Maximus ("Great Circus").

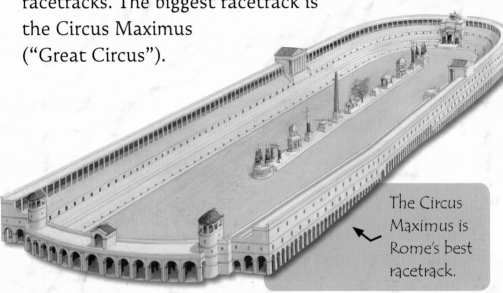

The Circus Maximus is Rome's best racetrack.

On race day, about 200,000 people sit around the track. Men and women sit together. Entry is free. Arrive early to get a seat.

CHOOSE YOUR TEAM

The teams and their colours are:
- the Russata team – red
- the Albata team – white
- the Veneta team – blue
- the Prasina team – green

Choose a team to support (see box on this page). Wear something in your team's colour. This shows who you support.

A DAY AT THE RACES

The day starts with a parade (show). You can see the **charioteers** and their chariots. Charioteers are the people who drive the chariots. Then it's race-time. About twelve chariots take part in a race. They go at speeds of up to 75 kph.

Chariot racing is dangerous. You may see a crash or pile-up. Horses and drivers are often badly hurt. Some are even killed.

Each race only lasts ten minutes. In between races, there is more entertainment. Watch acrobats. They ride the horses fast. Then they jump onto other moving horses!

The winner of a chariot race holds a leaf from a palm tree.

GO TO THE GAMES!

Ancient Roman games are a great show. But they are violent and bloody. Men called **gladiators** fight each other. Men fight wild animals. **Criminals** are killed at the games. This all happens in the Colosseum. This is a huge outdoor theatre.

In ancient Rome, gladiators are like superstars.

THE GAMES ARE COMING!

People paint notices on walls. These tell you that the games are coming. The games are very popular. Get your ticket early.

A DAY AT THE GAMES

- **Morning**: animal hunters kill lions, tigers, rhinoceroses, and other types of wild beasts.
- **Midday**: criminals are fed to the beasts.
- **Afternoon**: men fight to the death in gladiator contests.

WATCHING THE ACTION

There will be about 50,000 people in the Colosseum. Everyone will be very excited. Find your seat. Look down at the sandy floor where the games take place. The sand soaks up blood from injured people or animals! The games last all day. Take plenty of food and drink.

SIGN LANGUAGE

A gladiator falls to the ground. The winner stands over him. The crowd use their thumbs to make signs to the winner. These signs tell the winner what to do with the loser. Or the crowd calls out:

- *Hoc habet!* – Get him!
- *Mitte!* – Let him go!
- *Iugula!* – Kill him!

These are the ruins of the Roman **Forum**.

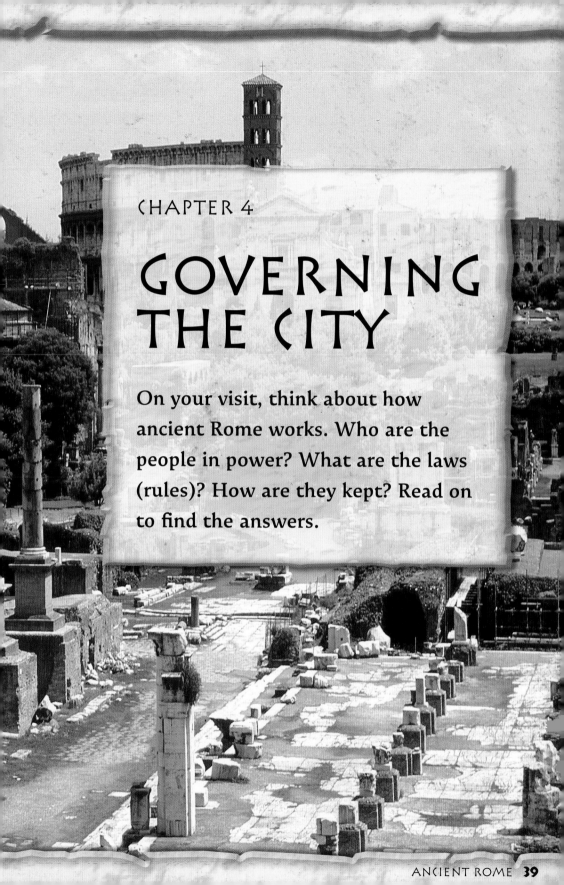

CHAPTER 4

GOVERNING THE CITY

On your visit, think about how ancient Rome works. Who are the people in power? What are the laws (rules)? How are they kept? Read on to find the answers.

RULERS OF ANCIENT ROME

At first, kings ruled ancient Rome. But they were cruel to ordinary people. About 2,500 years ago, a **government** took over power. A government is made up of people who run the country. The new government was called a **republic**. A republic does not have a king or queen.

The republic was run by a group of men called **senators**. The group was called the Senate. Senators are **elected** or chosen by vote.

For many years, there were battles for power. People tried to take power away from the Senate.

This is a statue of the emperor Augustus. Augustus was a good ruler.

GOOD AND BAD EMPERORS

The emperors ruling Rome since Augustus have been a mix of good and bad:

Emperor	Reigned	Good or bad?	Reason
Augustus	27 BC–AD 14	Good	Began rebuilding ancient Rome.
Caligula	AD 37–41	Bad	Wasted money.
Nero	AD 54–68	Bad	Murdered his mother and attacked Christians.
Trajan	AD 98–117	Good	The Roman Empire grew under his rule.
Marcus Aurelius	AD 161–180	Good	Thoughtful and popular.
Commodus	AD 180–192	Bad	Tried to rename ancient Rome after himself.

About 2,000 years ago, a man called Augustus took over. He governed the Roman Empire with the Senate. He called himself the **emperor**. This was the beginning of the Roman Empire.

THE EMPEROR'S BODYGUARD

The emperor has his own army. They are called the Praetorian Guard. This army keeps the emperor and the city of Rome safe from danger.

LAW AND ORDER

The ancient Romans are proud of their laws (rules). They believe they are the fairest in the world. It took the ancient Romans hundreds of years to work out their laws.

A SYSTEM OF PUNISHMENTS

If you break the law, this is what could happen.

- For the crime of stealing: The victim can decide what happens to you. The victim is the person who suffered the crime. You may have to pay a fine. Or you may receive a beating.

Senators who run the country decide on the laws.

- For the crime of murder: You are sent to court. This is where people decide what happens to you. A group of people called a **jury** listen to the facts of the crime. They decide if you are innocent or guilty. If you are innocent you can go home.

A wild animal kills a man.

If the jury says you are guilty (that you carried out the crime), your punishment may be:

- Exile from the city (sent to a faraway part of the Roman Empire)
- Death by beheading – cutting off your head
- Death by **impalement** — sticking a sharp stick through your body
- Death by fighting wild animals in the arena (see page 36).

The golden rule for visitors is: stay out of trouble!

Rich people spend lots of money on their villas.

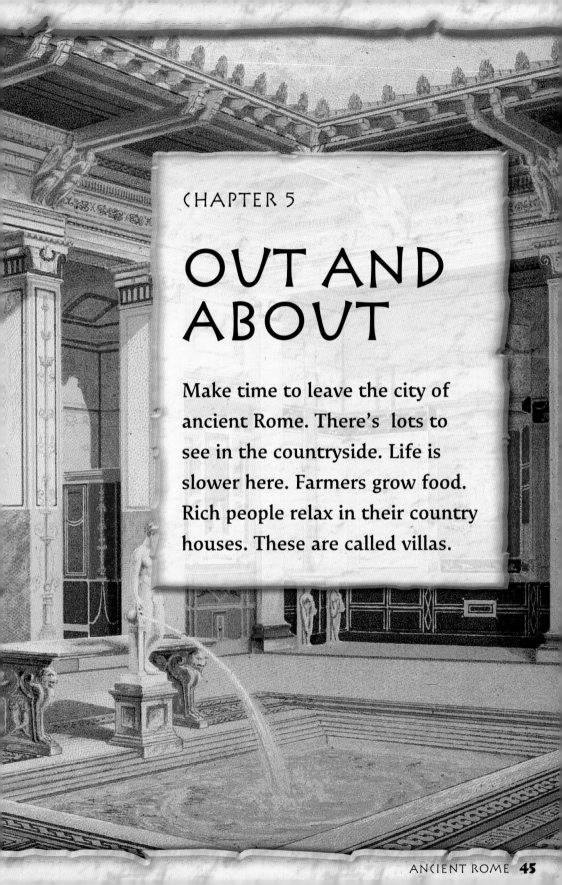

CHAPTER 5

OUT AND ABOUT

Make time to leave the city of ancient Rome. There's lots to see in the countryside. Life is slower here. Farmers grow food. Rich people relax in their country houses. These are called villas.

CHOOSE YOUR TRANSPORT

Walking is the cheapest way to get to the countryside. It also takes the longest! You can rent or buy a horse. You can find them in the stables in the city. Check to be sure the horse is fit and healthy.

CARRIAGES

Carriages cost more than horses. They are much more comfortable, though!

A husband and wife travel with the driver in a carriage.

The best carriage has four wheels. Four horses pull it along. It's a relaxing way to travel. You have your own driver. There's plenty of room for you and your luggage. Sit back and enjoy!

DANGER IN THE DARK

Don't travel when it is dark. There are many dangers. Thieves may attack you. They may steal your money. And they may even steal your clothes! So find somewhere to stay the night instead.

The fastest way to travel is in a two–wheeled carriage. Two horses pull this. The driver makes stops on the way. He can swap the tired horses for fresh ones. This means you can travel about 80 kilometres (50 miles) in ten hours.

TRAVEL IN STYLE

You can travel in a **litter**. This is a wooden box with a seat. There are windows and curtains. You need about eight men to carry it. These men are called bearers.

The litter is very slow. But it does look good! People with lots of money like travelling in a litter.

VISIT A VILLA

The city's richest people have villas or houses in the countryside. So do poor farmers. The farmer's villa is a working farm. A rich person's villa is much larger. It is a holiday home. Here people from the city enjoy the quiet countryside.

Simple farm villa

LIVING IN LUXURY

If you visit a rich person's villa, you will be treated like a special guest. A servant will look after you. You will eat a good meal with the owner.

The largest villas are like small villages. They have bakeries, dining rooms, and store rooms. There are bath-houses and large gardens. They are decorated with wall paintings and **mosaics** (see box on page 49).

Rich man's villa

PICTURES IN STONE

Mosaics are pictures on the floors and walls. They are made from small coloured cubes of stone. They can also be made from pottery or glass.

A teacher gives a boy a school lesson.

CHAPTER 6

CHILDREN IN ANCIENT ROME

The city of ancient Rome is a great place for children. Ancient Roman children play lots of different games. They also have toys. Boys from rich families often go to school as well.

FROM TOYS TO TEACHERS

Children play with rag dolls. They have model animals made from pottery. They also play with spinning tops, hoops, and building bricks. All children know how to play "flashing fingers". Learn the rules (see box below). Then you can play too.

FLASHING FINGERS

1 Agree on the number of points needed to win the game.
2 Stand in front of the other person.
3 On the count of three, both lift up your right hands. Stretch out some fingers.
4 As you lift your hands, you both call out a number. This can be between 0 – 10.
5 If the number you call matches the number of fingers you both showed, score a point.
6 The person who has the most points wins.

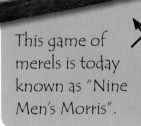

HEADS OR SHIPS?

To decide who goes first in a game, children toss an old coin. They call out "capita" ("heads") or "navia" ("ships"). Old coins have a picture of a ship on the "tail" side.

This game of merels is today known as "Nine Men's Morris".

GOING TO SCHOOL

In ancient Rome, only boys from rich families go to school. Girls stay at home. They learn how to cook and make clothes. They learn how to look after the family.

School starts at dawn. It finishes in the early afternoon. At school, boys learn to read and write in Greek and Latin. They study arithmetic and history. They also study the stars. This is called **astronomy**.

These children roll nuts in a game.

Teachers are harsh. They punish naughty children. They punish children who get things wrong!

WHEN CHILDHOOD ENDS

A boy becomes a man on his 16th birthday. This is a very important day. He takes part in a ceremony. This celebrates his "coming of age". From then on, he can do all the things a man can do.

A girl "comes of age" at fourteen. Then she can marry. She can start her own family.

This is a 20th-century artist's idea of the Roman **Forum**.

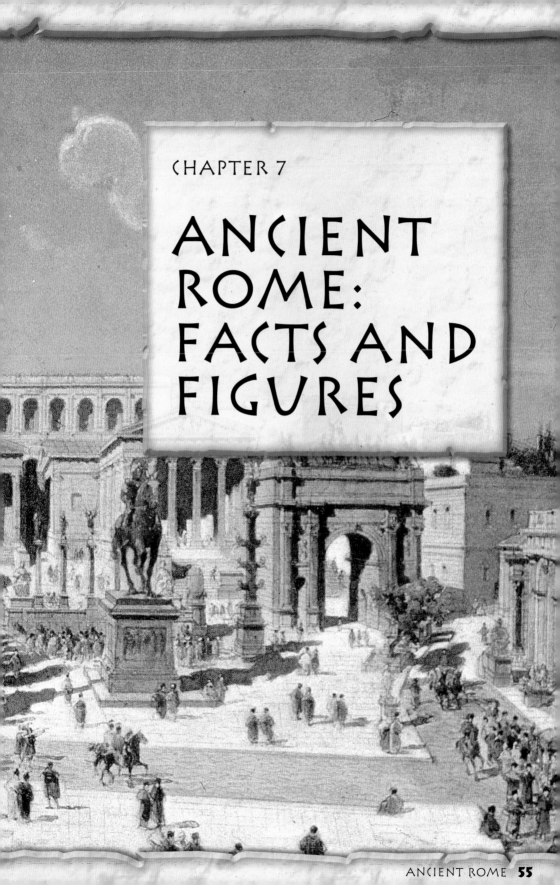

CHAPTER 7

ANCIENT ROME: FACTS AND FIGURES

LATIN PHRASEBOOK

These words and phrases will be useful on your visit. To say them correctly, say every letter in the word as it is written. "C" should sound like a "k", and "v" should sound like a "w".

GENERAL LATIN PHRASES

Hello	*Salve* (but *Salvete* if you are talking to more than one person)
Goodbye	*Vale* (but *Valete* if you are talking to more than one person)
Thank you	*Gratias ago vobis*
Yes/No	*Ita/Non*
Good/Bad	*Bonus/Malus*
I would like…	*Velim…*
How much?	*Quantus?*
How many?	*Quot?*
Where?	*Ubi?*
When?	*Quando?*
What?	*Quod?*
What is this?	*Quid hoc est?*
How do I get to…?	*Qua via venio ad…?*
Is it far?	*Est ne longinquum?*
Where are the lions?	*Ubi sunt leones?*
I am hungry.	*Esurio.*

USEFUL LATIN WORDS

FOOD

Bread	*Panis*
Cheese	*Caseus*
Eggs	*Ova*
Fish	*Piscis*
Fruit	*Pomum*
Meat	*Caro*
Milk	*Lac*
Sausage	*Botulus*
Vegetables	*Holera*
Water	*Aqua*

DAYS OF THE WEEK

ROMAN DAY	MEANING	YOUR DAY
Dies Solis	Day of the Sun	Sunday
Dies Lunae	Day of the Moon	Monday
Dies Martis	Day of Mars	Tuesday
Dies Mercuris	Day of Mercury	Wednesday
Dies Iovis	Day of Jupiter	Thursday
Dies Veneris	Day of Venus	Friday
Dies Saturni	Day of Saturn	Saturday

ROMAN NUMBERS

Roman numerals (numbers written down) are made up from mixtures of the following seven letters:

I = 1   V = 5   X = 10   L = 50   C = 100   D = 500
M = 1,000

Large numbers become more difficult.
Use these rules to help:

1 Numbers are written in a line.

2 Numbers start with the biggest numeral (on the left) and work down to the smallest (on the right).

Here are two examples:

- LXXXVIII 50 + 10 + 10 + 10 + 5 + 1 + 1 + 1 = 88
- LXXXIX   50 + 10 + 10 + 10 + (10-1) = 89

ANCIENT ROMAN NUMBERS

Number	Numeral	Latin name	Number	Numeral	Latin name
1	I	unus	20	XX	viginti
2	II	duo	30	XXX	triginta
3	III	tres	40	XL	quadraginta
4	IV	quattuor	50	L	quinquaginta
5	V	quinque	100	C	centum
6	VI	sex	200	CC	decenti
7	VII	septem	300	CCC	trecenti
8	VIII	octo	400	CD	quadringenti
9	IX	novem	500	D	quingenti
10	X	decem	1,000	M	mille

FESTIVALS AND GLADIATORS

SOME ANCIENT ROMAN FESTIVALS

Month	Festival name	Festival description
February	*Parentalia*	In honour of family members who lived in the past.
March	*Fordicidia*	Marks the start of the farming year.
June	*Vestalia*	In honour of Vesta, goddess of the home.
October	*Fontinalia*	Festival of water.
November	*Ludi Plebeii*	Festival of games.
December	*Saturnalia*	In honour of the god Saturn.

GLADIATORS – THE ONES TO WATCH

- **Andabata** ("blind-fighter") – wears a helmet without eyeholes. Finds his enemy by feeling around.
- **Hoplomachus** ("shield-fighter") – fights with a long pole with a pointed end and a short sword.
- **Laquerarius** ("noose-fighter") – fights with a lasso.
- **Retiarius** ("net-fighter") – fights with a net, a three-pronged fork, and a long dagger.
- **Secutor** ("chaser") – carries a large shield and fights with a dagger or short sword.

ANCIENT ROME AT A GLANCE

TIMELINE

(BC means the years before our modern calendar started. AD is the time of our modern calendar.)

about 1000 BC	First villages on the seven hills of Rome.
753 BC	According to legends (stories), the beginning of Rome.
about 753–509 BC	Rome ruled by kings.
509 BC	Last king overthrown; Roman **Republic** begins.
264 BC	First **gladiatorial** (men fighting in games) contest in Rome.
264–146 BC	Wars against North Africa and Greece.
59–51 BC	Gaul is conquered.
45 BC	Caesar rules Rome.
44 BC	Caesar killed for being too powerful.
27 BC	Roman Republic ends. Roman **Empire** begins. Augustus is the first Roman Emperor.
AD 43	Conquest of Britain begins.
AD 64	Fire destroys much of Rome. Nero attacks Christians.
AD 68–69	Nero dies. Power struggles lead to war.
AD 79	Roman towns destroyed by the volcano (mountain exploding with hot rock) Vesuvius.
AD 80	Colosseum opens in Rome.
about AD 120	Roman Empire at its largest.
AD 120–128	Hadrian's Wall built in Britain.
AD 284	Roman Empire split into Eastern and Western parts.
AD 313	Christianity and other religions are accepted in the Roman Empire.

AD 330	Constantinople (Istanbul) becomes the "New Rome" in the east, capital of the Roman world.
about AD 400	Last known gladiatorial contest at the Colosseum.
AD 410	Rome attacked by Goths.
AD 476	Romulus Augustulus gives up his title. He is the last emperor of the Western Empire.
AD 476–1453	Eastern Empire is successful for 1,000 years. Then the Turks take over Constantinople.

FURTHER READING

BOOKS

Ancient Rome, Peter Connolly and Andrew Solway (Oxford University Press, 2001)

Illustrated Encyclopedia of Ancient Rome, Mike Corbishley (British Museum, 2003)

WEBSITES

- www.thebritishmuseum.ac.uk/world/rome/rome.html
  Search for items in the British Museum collection.
- www.maquettes-historiques.net/P5.html
  Superb model of the City of Rome — don't miss this one!
- www.crystalinks.com/romeclothing.html
  Clothes in ancient Rome.

GLOSSARY

amphitheatre outdoor theatre used for games and events

ancestor family member who lived in the past

astronomy study of the stars and planets and their movements

banquet great feast with many different courses of food

basilica shopping centre with offices and law courts

chamber pot a bowl used as a toilet

chariot type of fast-moving carriage or cart

charioteer a person who drives a chariot in races

criminal a person who has carried out a crime

elected when a person is chosen by vote for a particular job

empire group of countries all ruled by the same government

emperor the head of the countries that make up the empire

forum open space in a town or city, where public meetings, festivals, and processions are held

gladiator man trained to fight in a certain way for public entertainment

government people who are in charge of a country

impalement being stuck on a sharp object

jury group of people at a trial who decide whether a person is guilty or not guilty of a crime

litter type of seat for a single person carried by a group of bearers on their shoulders

mosaic picture on the floor or wall made from small pieces of coloured stone, glass, or clay

multicultural society in which people of all races and religions live together

politician person involved in politics, the business of running a country

republic government in which ordinary people choose their leaders

sacred place or object that is thought to be holy

sacrifice to make offerings, such as food, to a god. Sometimes animals are killed for this purpose.

senator member of the Senate, which was the governing body of Rome

sewer underground drain that carries away waste from toilets

temple building used for religious events and ceremonies

toga loose cloak worn by men for much of Roman history

tragedy drama about serious and often disastrous events

warrior a person who fights in battle

INDEX